Home Made Dog Treat Recipes

Book Two

Karen J Connell

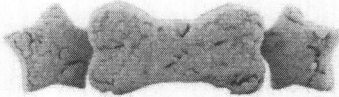

Front Cover Photo: The very handsome Gryphon – owned and photographed by Evelynn Paula Gibson

Back Cover Photo: Talkative Jimmy – owned by Paula and Jasmin Thompson (photograph by 8 year old Jasmin Thompson)

Martin Clunes with cutie Amber (Lawleymoon Shine on Siouxline) - owned by Judy Manley

Thank you to everyone who allowed me to use photographs of their much loved pets.

Many of the photographs in this book are much loved family pets and the photographs are mostly taken by their owners.

Contents

Introduction

Thank you for buying Book Two in the 'Homemade Dog Treat Recipes' series.

Book One is available at **www.bit.ly/dtreats**

As with the first book, I will be donating a chunk of any profits made from the sales of this book to a dog rescue charity each month.

The people who spend their time and money helping stray, abused and desperate dogs deserve our unending admiration and we can help in a small way by donating a little towards their causes.

By the very fact that you are reading this book I'm guessing you have a least one dog of your own and if, like me, you want your 'best friend' to have the best you can give him, have a go at making some of the treats in this book.

Making your own dog treats has many advantages over store bought treats.

For example:

- You get to use any ingredients your dog likes and leave out stuff that is not good for him.

- If your dog has preferences, like blackberries (my girl delicately picks her own from the bushes when they are in season...), you can make biscuit treats including them or make doggy muffins with blackberries. If he loves sardines, there are lots of great recipes that could include them. You can give him exactly what he likes best.

- Your dog may have an intolerance to some types of flour so you can use a substitute and know the treats you make will not cause him any unpleasant side effects.

- With homemade dog treats you control the quality of any ingredients you use.

- You can use the same ingredients that you would use for your own family and always know the ingredients are healthy, good quality and safe for your dog and without fillers and preservatives.

- You can produce just as many or as few of the treats as you want to make. You can increase or decrease the quantities of a recipe to suit your own dogs. When I am making treats I have not made before I usually make a small batch to begin with to see if my dogs like them or to check they don't have an allergic reaction to any of the ingredients.

- In most cases when you make treats yourself you will end up saving money because you can buy ingredients in bulk or when they are cheaper.

- You can prepare your treats for the oven and pop them in when you are cooking for the family.

- If your dog has any allergies, you can make sure that you only use ingredients that are safe for your dog to eat and avoid using any items that might trigger a reaction in your dog.

- You can make your treats healthier than shop bought treats by using 'good' fats rather than saturated fats. If you have read the first **Dog Treat book** (www.bit.ly/dtreats) in this series you will know that I am a big fan of using coconut oil in my recipes rather than butter. I also leave out any salt or sugar in the hope that my dogs will remain healthy and fit.

Yet another advantage of making your own dog treats is that you can adapt any of the recipes in this book to include stuff your dog likes but remember not to include things that are not good for him.

Some of those that are NOT good are below but please **do your own research**:

- Raisins, grapes, currants etc.
- Onions
- Chocolate
- Alcohol
- Apple seeds (peel and core any apples fed to your dog)
- Chewing gum (contains Xylitol which is poisonous for dogs)
- Coffee
- Avocado

For more information on foods **not** to feed your dogs and why these ingredients are forbidden, visit this page **www.bit.ly/dogpoisons**

Warning - When you buy peanut butter to add to your dog treat recipes, please be aware that there are peanut butter manufacturers adding xylitol to their ingredients. Check the label of the brand you intend to buy to make absolutely sure xylitol is **NOT** included in the ingredient list.

If in doubt - leave it out!

Vegetables contain loads of minerals and vitamins that are good for both man and animal and most dogs love them. I add shredded vegetables to almost any dog treat recipe that I make - nothing is wasted in my house.

Don't throw away vegetables or fruit that is nearing its 'sell by' date, shred or finely chop it (remembering to remove pips or seeds first) then freeze it for the next time you make your dog treats. Do the same with end bits of cheese - most dogs love cheese.

If your dog has weight issues, you can make treats that do not contain lots of fattening oils and sugars.

Please do remember that treats are supposed to be just that – a TREAT, not a meal or fed continuously throughout the day.

Some of the recipes include bouillon granules but I like to use a homemade stock instead because I find a lot of the granules are just too salty.

If you have boiled a few vegetables for the family dinner, save the liquid rather than throw it away and use it in your Dog Treat recipes. Or cook a piece of chicken by boiling in water for 5 -10 minutes in a saucepan. Save the stock (freeze if not needed immediately), cool the chicken and slice for your lunchtime sandwich and you have a delicious healthy lunch for yourself and some great stock for your dog treats. You could also boil the bones from a chicken carcass to make a stock.

There are a few recipes in this book for complete meals for fussy eaters or those recovering from illness and need encouraging to eat.

At the end of this book I have included a conversion chart so you can easily convert from US weights to imperial measures. I hope you find this useful.

So let's get to the recipes.

My own, very precious, Paula

*"Every once in a while a dog enters your life
and changes everything"*

Simple Sardine Bites

Ingredients

1 can sardines in oil (or tomato sauce – up to you)
2 eggs
2 tbsp coconut oil
1 cup flour

Method

Preheat oven to 350°.

Put the 2 eggs and sardines, including oil and coconut oil into a food processor and blitz.

Add the flour and blitz again until the dough comes together. You may need to add more flour to get the right consistency.

Turn out onto a lightly floured board and roll out to desired thickness. Cut into shapes and place on lightly greased baking sheet.

Place in oven for around 10 – 15 minutes. Turn off the oven and leave in oven to cool and crisp up.

Basic Dog Treats

Ingredients

2 ½ cups flour of your choice
1 egg
1 tsp. beef or chicken Bouillon granules
½ cup hot water

Method

Preheat oven to 350°.

Dissolve the Bouillon in hot water.

Mix flour and egg.

Add the Bouillon to the mixture.

Knead until it forms a ball.

Roll out to ½ inch thickness.

Cut into desired shapes.

Place cut outs on lightly greased cookie sheet.

Bake for 15-20 minutes (or until done).

Carrot and Peanut Butter Delight

Ingredients

2 carrots
½ cup water
½ cup cooked brown rice
¼ cup peanut butter (check label for xylitol)
1 cup flour

Method

Preheat oven to 350°.

Cook rice according to directions and let it cool (left over rice works very well).

Wash and shred (grate) the carrots (no need to peel). Steam or boil for a few minutes.

Puree the carrots, peanut butter and rice.

Transfer to a bowl and mix in the flour. Next add enough water to form a dough.

Use a spoon or ice cream scoop to place the dough onto a lightly greased cookie sheet.

Bake for 15-20 minutes (soft and chewy center – ideal for those older dogs).

The adorable Scruffy and his pal Frankie – Owned
and photographed by Dulcie Ogilvie

"You are never alone if you have a dog – or two…"

Chicken and Yogurt Treat

This mixture is good for encouraging a fussy eater to eat his dinner. Simply drizzle a couple of spoonfuls over his regular meal.

Ingredients

3 oz. chicken breast
¼ - ½ cup water
¼ cup plain yogurt

Method

Cut chicken into very small cubes and boil in the water for around 5 minutes

Puree chicken cubes, water, and yogurt

Cool and serve by the spoonful

Unused portions can be frozen in ice cube trays or paper cupcake cases then stored in freezer bags

Meet these two very beautiful boys, Brody (front) and Blue
(back) - Owned and photographed by Cari Wickens

*"There is only one thing better than having a dog -
having two dogs."*

Pumpkin Balls

Ingredients

½ can canned pumpkin
4 tbsp. molasses – optional (I prefer to substitute with 2 eggs)
4 tbsp. water
2 tbsp. vegetable oil
2 cups flour (more if required)
¼ tsp baking powder

Method

Preheat oven to 350°.

Mix wet ingredients together in a bowl.

Mix flour and baking powder together then stir into wet ingredients until dough is soft enough to work.

Scoop small spoonful into your hand and roll into a ball (dampen hands to prevent sticking if necessary).

Place on lightly greased cookie sheet.

Flatten with a fork if you prefer a flat biscuit.

Bake for around 20-25 minutes and allow to cool before storing in airtight container. You can freeze for later use.

Apple Muffins

Ingredients

¼ cup apple sauce (unsweetened)
2 ¾ cups water
2 tbsp. honey
1/8 tbsp. vanilla extract
1 egg
4 cups flour
1 cup dried apple chips (avoid ones with artificial sweeteners)
1 tbsp. baking powder

Method

Preheat oven to 350°.

Mix first 5 ingredients in a bowl.

Add remaining ingredients and mix until blended.

Pour into lightly greased muffin pans – I use the small pans.

Bake for 45 minutes or until done.

This is the type of baking pan I use for dog muffins, they are smaller than regular muffin pans.

To see more – www.bit.ly/bakingpan

Peanut Butter Boost

Ingredients

1/3 cup peanut butter
2 cups flour
1 cup rolled oats
1 tbsp. honey
½ tablespoon fish oil or coconut oil (optional)
1½ cups water

Method

Preheat oven to 350°.

Mix flour and oats together.

Add 1 cup water and mix well.

Add peanut butter, honey, and oil and mix until well blended.

Slowly add remaining water until mixture becomes thick and doughy.

Roll the dough onto a lightly floured surface and roll to ¼ inch thickness.

Cut into the desired shapes.

Place on a baking sheet and bake for 40 minutes.

The very thoughtful Daisy – Owned and photographed by Anna Brodie

The Eyes are the Window to the Soul

Pot Roast Balls

Ingredients

1 cup flour
1 cup water (more if needed to puree the beef)
3 oz. cooked beef (Sunday lunch left overs are ideal)
1 carrot (washed)
½ cup cooked peas

Method

Puree the beef with ½ cup of water (add more 1 tbsp. at a time if needed)

Shred the carrot

Add the shredded carrot and peas to the beef mixture and puree

Transfer mixture to a bowl

Add flour and mix well.

Adjust mixture to desired consistency by adding more water or more flour

Wet your hands to prevent sticking, take some of the dough and roll into a ball. Place on a baking tray.

Cook for around 30 minutes.

Unused balls can be frozen.

Turkey and Vegetable Lunch

The next two recipes are not really a treat but a good and nutritious meal for when your dog need a bit of help encouraging him to eat or when recovering from an illness.

Ingredients

2 cups of water
½ pound of turkey
1 cup of brown rice
½ cup of chopped carrots
½ cup of chopped green beans

Method

For this recipe you could use turkey chopped into cubes or ground (minced) turkey.

Add brown rice, turkey, and water to a large pot and bring to a boil.

Reduce heat to medium-low and cook for around 15 minutes.

Add carrots and green beans (or substitute for vegetables you know your dog likes) and cook for an additional 5 to 10 minutes adding more water if necessary.

Leftovers can be stored in the refrigerator for up to 5 days or frozen in ice cube trays and placed in a freezer bag.

Chicken Casserole

Ingredients

2 chicken breasts
¼ cup of green beans, chopped
¼ cup of carrots, chopped
¼ cup of broccoli, chopped
¼ cup rolled oats.
2 cups of water

Method

Trim excess fat from the chicken breasts and cut breasts into small pieces

Add chopped chicken and remaining ingredients to a large pot and simmer for around 15 minutes. Allow to cool before serving.

Introducing the very majestic Floyd – Owned by Myles Harris

(Photograph by Elizabeth Gibson)

You have treats? For Me?

Carrot & Oat Dog Biscuits

Ingredients

½ cup carrot juice
½ cup unsweetened applesauce
2 large eggs
3 tablespoons natural creamy peanut butter
2 teaspoons pure vanilla extract
2 cups all-purpose flour
½ cup coarsely ground cornmeal
½ cup rolled oats

Method

Preheat the oven to 400° Fahrenheit

Combine all ingredients in a large bowl and stir to form a thick dough. Transfer the dough onto a lightly floured surface.

Sprinkle flour on the dough while rolling to ¼" thickness.

Cut out desired shapes dipping the cutter into flour to help prevent sticking.

Transfer biscuits onto a cookie sheet lined with parchment paper (dough does not spread out during baking).

Bake for 20 minutes or until lightly brown.

Turn off oven and allow to cool in oven to crisp up.

Unused biscuits can be stored for in fridge for up to 5 days or in the freezer for longer.

Dog Rules

1. The dog is not allowed in the house.

2. OK, the dog is allowed in the house but only in certain rooms.

3. The dog is allowed in all rooms but has to stay off the furniture.

4. The dog can get on the old furniture only.

5. Fine, the dog is allowed on all furniture, but is not allowed to sleep with humans on the bed.

6. OK, the dog is allowed on the bed but only by invitation.

7. The dog can sleep on the bed whenever he wants but not under the covers.

8. The dog can sleep under the covers by invitation only.

9. The dog can sleep under the covers anytime.

10. Humans must ask permission to sleep under the covers with the dog.

~ Author Unknown

Banana Oatmeal Cookies

Ingredients

1 ripe banana
2 tbsp. coconut oil
1 cup instant oatmeal

Instructions

Preheat oven to 350° Fahrenheit.

In medium sized bowl, mix instant oatmeal according to instructions.

Mash the ripe banana into the oatmeal. Mix in the coconut oil.

Form into serving size balls and transfer onto a lightly greased cookie sheet.

Flatten with a fork. Bake for roughly 15 minutes. Cool and serve.

Very handsome Paxi – Owned and photographed by Lie Florus

The Russian Spy look…

Veggie Cookies

Ingredients

1 cup pumpkin puree
¼ cup peanut butter
2 large eggs
½ cup old fashioned oats
3 cups whole wheat flour (more if needed)
1 small carrot
1 small zucchini
1 cup chopped spinach (you can substitute any of the vegetables with those your dog prefers)

Method

Preheat oven to 350° Fahrenheit.

Mix the first three ingredients with a food processor.

Slowly add the oats and 2½ cups flour. Add remaining flour, ¼ cup at a time until dough is no longer sticky.

Add shredded carrot, zucchini, and spinach to the mixer (careful not to over mix).

On a lightly floured surface, knead the dough until it comes together and roll to ¼ inch thickness.

Cut out desired shapes and place onto a lightly greased baking sheet.

Bake for 20-25 minutes.

Cool and serve.

After I've Gone... *Eugene O'Neill's Last Will and Testament of a Dog*
(adapted).

Before humans die they write their last will and testament, giving their home and all they have to those they leave behind.

If, with my paws, I could do the same, this is what I'd ask...

To a poor lonely stray, I'd give place in our happy home, my bowl, my cozy bed, my soft pillow and all my toys.

I would give the lap which I so love to sit on, the hand that gently stroked my fur and the loving voice that spoke my name. I would give the fun and laughter I shared with you in our home, on our walks and our days out.

I'd will to the sad, scared shelter dog the place I had in your loving heart and my place by your side.

So, when I die, please do not say, "I will never have a dog again, for the loss and pain is more than I can stand."

Instead, please go and find an unloved dog (or two), whose life has held no kindness, or hope, and give my place to him.

This is the only thing I can give - the love I leave behind.

Veggie Smoothie

Ingredients

1 carrot
1 zucchini
½ cup spinach
½ cup plain yogurt (or favorite flavor but no artificial sweeteners)
1 tsp. honey
¼ cup water

Method

Wash all the vegetables.

Puree in a blender.

Add additional water to desired consistency.

Spoon over their favorite dog food or in an individual treat dish.

Leftovers can be stored in the refrigerator for up to 5 days or frozen in ice cube trays and placed in freezer bags.

This is also a good recipe for freezing in cupcake cases and giving to your dog frozen when the weather is hot.

Allow to sit for a few minutes after you take out of freezer before giving to your dog.

Bacon Supreme

Ingredients

2 ½ cups flour (plus more if needed)
1 tbsp. baking powder
1 cup cooked turkey bacon, crumbled
¼ cup shredded cheddar cheese
1 cup milk

Method

Preheat oven to 350°

Mix flour and baking powder in a large bowl

Stir in remaining ingredients until a soft dough forms (add more flour if needed)

Use your hands to make appropriate sized dough balls for your dog

Place balls on a cookie sheet and cook for 20 minutes, flipping half way through

Cool before serving

Unused portions can be stored in the refrigerator for up to 5 days or in a freezer bag in the freezer

Basic Baked Peanut Butter Treats

Ingredients

1 ½ cups flour
½ cup peanut butter
¼ cup oats
¼ cup grated carrots
Pinch of cinnamon
1 tsp. baking powder
¼ cup water

Method

Preheat oven to 350°

Combine ingredients

Roll to ¼ inch thickness

Cut out with cookie cutters

Bake for 10 minutes

Flip cookies over and bake until golden brown

Cool and serve.

The lovely Nuba – Owned and photographed by Anita Breznik

"Now where did that rabbit get to?"

Healthy Training Treats

Ingredients

2 chicken breasts (excess fat trimmed)
1 cup cooked rice

Method

Preheat oven to 350° Fahrenheit

Cut the chicken into bite size pieces and puree in a blender – it will be very sticky

Transfer sticky mixture to a large bowl and stir in the cooked rice

Using plastic gloves, roll the mixture and cut into small shapes

Place on a greased cookie sheet

Bake for 10 minutes, turn them over and finish baking until golden brown (usually another 10 minutes)

Cool completely before serving

Store unused portions in the fridge for up to 5 days or transfer to a freezer bag and keep for longer

The very cute Billy with his feline friend – owned and photographed by Trish Gilbert

"A house without either a cat or a dog is the house of a scoundrel." - Portuguese Proverb

The Golden Bone

Ingredients

2 eggs, divided (1 for the dough, 1 for the wash)
1 tbsp. vegetable oil
2 tsp. honey
½ cup chicken stock
½ cup whole wheat flour
1/3 cup all-purpose flour (more if needed)
¼ cup cornmeal (polenta or maize flour for UK cooks)
½ cup peanut butter

Method

Preheat the oven to 325°.

In a large bowl, whisk together 1 egg, the oil and honey. Whisk in the chicken stock. Using a processor, combine the two flours and cornmeal.

Slowly pour in the chicken stock mixture, then add the peanut butter. Mix until the dough comes together.

Roll out the dough to around ½ inch thickness. Cut into shapes using a bone shaped cutter. Place on baking sheets sprayed with cooking oil.

Whisk the remaining egg and brush the egg wash lightly over the cookies.

Let it stand for about 10 minutes and brush them with egg mixture again (gives baked cookies a delicious color).

Bake until golden brown, roughly 15 minutes.

A Promise to My Dog...

I Promise...

...I will never move and not take you with me
...I will never put you in a shelter and leave
...I will never let you be hungry
...I will never let you be hurt
...I will never desert you when you get old
...I will never leave you when you go blind
...if that time comes I will be there to hold you

Because you are family and I love you

Flax and Turmeric Biscuits

Ingredients

¾ cup hot water
1 tsp. beef or chicken bouillon powder (*you could substitute the water and bouillon powder for homemade chicken stock*)
1 ½ cups all-purpose flour
1 cup whole wheat flour
2 tbsp. brown sugar
½ cup ground flax seed
1 tbsp. turmeric
½ cup peanut butter
1 egg

Method

Preheat the oven to 350°

Dissolve bouillon in hot water.

Use a mixer to combine the next 5 ingredients in a large bowl.

Switch to the dough hook and add the hot water mixture, peanut butter and egg.

Mix until the dough ball is smooth.

Roll out the dough to ½ inch thick.

Cut into desired dog biscuit shapes.

Transfer the biscuits to a cookie sheet lined with parchment paper.

Bake for about 35 minutes or until the biscuits feel dried and fairly hard (they will harden a bit more after cooling).

Cool completely before serving.

**Every child should have two things;
A dog, and a Mother willing to let him
have one...**

Peanut Butter Drops

Ingredients

1½ cups peanut butter
½ ripe banana
¼ cup plain yogurt
Water as needed

Method

Mash the banana in a medium size mixing bowl

Add the peanut butter and yogurt Mix well (add water if dough is too thick)

Use a small scoop (or tablespoon) and scoop onto a cookie sheet lined with parchment paper

For a little extra fun, push a small dog bone biscuit treat into the drop

Freeze for several hours then transfer into a freezer bag and freeze overnight.

Leave for 5 minutes or so before serving. These are a nice treat for when the weather is hot.

I use small paper cases like these available on Amazon:

Roly doing a great photobomb – owned by Samantha and Dominc Ghiotti

Photograph taken by Dominic Ghiotti

Cheesy Mashed Potato Discs

Ingredients

1 cup of leftover mashed potatoes (not instant potatoes)
¼ cup of grated cheese
2 tbsp flour

Method

Preheat oven to 300°

Mix the flour into the mashed potatoes then mix in the grated cheese

Roll into marble size balls, place on baking sheet then flatten.

Cook for around 10 minutes then turn off oven leaving the discs in the oven while they cool.

Store in an airtight container in the fridge or freeze for later.

Puppy Patties

Ingredients

½ lb. of lean ground (minced) meat – chicken, beef, turkey etc.

¼ cup shredded (grated) carrots

¼ cup shredded cheese

Method

Preheat oven to 350° Fahrenheit

Put the meat in a medium sized bowl, add the carrots and cheese and mix together.

Roll into appropriate sized balls depending on size of your dog.

Place on a cookie sheet and flatten slightly.

Bake for 20 minutes, turn, bake another 5 minutes or until thoroughly cooked

Cool completely before serving

Leftover patties can be stored in the fridge for up to 5 days or in an airtight container in the freezer.

Rice and Chicken Comfort Bites

This is great for if your dog is not well or needs to be encouraged to eat.

Ingredients

Water as needed
1 chicken breast, diced into small pieces
½ cup of rice
1 tsp. ground flaxseed

Method

Boil the chicken in water for around 2 minutes. Drain and save the water.

Cook the rice according to directions using the chicken stock you saved.

Transfer the rice to a medium size mixing bowl.

Add a small amount of water and mash the rice to a pudding like consistency

Stir in the finely diced cooked chicken and flaxseed

Cool completely and serve

The very angelic Jasper in his new sweater – owned and
photographed by Donna Blake

Coconut Bites

Ingredients

1/3 cup coconut oil
2-3 tbsp. peanut butter
2½ cups rolled oats
1/3 cup finely shredded coconut

Method

Place the coconut in a small bowl and set aside

Mix first 3 ingredients together thoroughly in a bowl.

Using your hands, roll dough into bite sized pieces

Roll each ball in the coconut Place on a flat tray lined with baking paper

Refrigerate for 30 minutes

You can serve immediately or freeze for later.

Rufus being thoughtful – owned and photographed by
Graham Hughes

Great Ginger Cookies

Ingredients

2 cups almond flour
½ cup Coconut Flour
¾ cup peanut butter
3 tablespoons ground ginger
1 tablespoon cinnamon
¼ cup water

Method

Preheat oven to 325° Fahrenheit

Mix all ingredients in a large bowl

Form a ball with the dough

Roll the dough to ½ inch thickness

Cut out desired shapes

Transfer shapes onto lightly greased cookie sheet and bake for 25 minutes

If desired, turn oven off and leave in the oven for another 30 minutes for a crispy cookie.

Two Ingredient Buster Biscuits

Ingredients

2 cups whole wheat flour (or wheat germ, spelt, rolled oats — or a mixture of these)
2 jars of pureed baby food – sweet or savory, it's your choice.

Method

Preheat oven to 350°.

Mix ingredients together to form a stiff dough. Add extra flour or water if needed to get the right consistency.

On a lightly floured surface, roll dough out evenly until it's about ¼ inch thick. Use cookie cutters to cut into desired shape or a pizza cutter to make cubes the right size for your dog. Lightly grease a cookie sheet, place treats about ½ inch apart. Bake for 20 – 25 minutes.

Turn off the oven and allow to cool completely. You can make a lot of these biscuits and freeze for later. The dough also freezes well too so, if you make a big batch of dough you can freeze it and make more biscuits later.

Don't forget you can add all sorts of tasty surprises like shredded (grated) carrots, cheese or sweet potatoes, parsley for fresh breath, blueberries, bananas, etc., whatever non-toxic fruits or vegetables your dog likes.

Apple Cheddar Muffins

Ingredients

1 cup all-purpose flour
½ cup whole wheat flour
¼ cup old fashioned rolled oats
2 teaspoons baking powder
½ teaspoon baking soda
½ cup applesauce (unsweetened)
½ cup water
¼ cup vegetable oil
1 tablespoon honey
2 eggs
1 apple (peeled, sliced, diced SEEDS REMOVED)
1 cup grated cheese (cheddar)

Method

Preheat oven to 400° Fahrenheit

Line muffin tins with paper liners.

In a large bowl mix the first four ingredients

In a medium bowl, whisk together the applesauce, water, oil, honey and eggs Stir in the apple and cheese

Add the wet ingredients to the flour mixture and stir (do not over mix)

Spoon the batter into the muffin tins

Bake for 15 to 20 minutes. Cool before serving

For me a house or an apartment becomes a home when you add one set of four legs, a happy, waggy tail and that indescribable measure of love that we call a dog

~ Roger Caras

Cinnamon and Peanut Butter Bones

Ingredients

2 cups oats
1½ cups brown rice flour
1¼ teaspoons ground cinnamon
1 cup fresh parsley leaves or ½ cup dried parsley
1 egg
2 tbsp peanut butter
1 tbsp coconut oil
½ cup low-salt chicken broth or water

Method

Place the oats in a food processor fitted with the metal blade. Process until finely chopped.

Add the brown rice flour, baking soda and cinnamon and process until blended.Add the parsley and process until blended.

Add the egg, peanut butter, coconut oil and process until blended.

Add the chicken broth or water a little at a time and process just until the mixture comes together to form a dough.

Transfer the dough to a large piece of plastic wrap and roll out to ½ inch thickness (if the rolling pin sticks, you could also cover the dough with the plastic wrap).

We Adopted Your Dog Today...

We adopted your dog today, the one you left at the pound,

The one you had for two years and no longer wanted around.

We adopted your dog today, did you know he's lost weight?

Did you know he's scared and depressed and has no idea what is his fate?

We adopted your dog today, he had fleas and a little cold

Guess you don't care what shape he's in, you abandoned him so I'm told

We adopted your dog today, were you having a baby or moving away?

Did you suddenly develop allergies or did you just not want him to stay?

We adopted your dog today, he doesn't play or eat much

I guess he's very sad inside and he really needs a kind touch

We adopted your dog today, and here he is going to stay

He's found his forever home and a warm bed in which to lay.

We adopted your dog today and we shall give him all he'll need

Patience, Love and Security so he can forget your selfish deed...

Puppy's Bed

Now I lay me down to sleep,
The king-size bed is soft and deep.
I sleep right in the centre groove,
My human grumbles she can hardly move.

I've trapped her legs, she's tucked in tight,
And here is where I pass the night.
No one disturbs me or dares intrude
Till morning comes and I want food.

I sneak up slowly to begin,
My nibbles on my human's chin.
She wakes up quickly,
I've stood on her knee
I'm a puppy, don't you see?

The morning is here and it's time to play
Nothing is going to get in my way.
So thank you Lord for giving me,
This human person that I see.
The one who hugs me and holds me tight,
And sacrifices her bed at night.

Honey and Oat Crunchies

Ingredients

½ cup of peanut butter (I used the smooth kind)
¼ cup honey
1 tbsp of virgin coconut oil (or olive oil)
1 cup chicken broth
1 cup rolled oats
1 cup whole wheat flour
1 cup all-purpose flour

Method

Preheat oven to 350°.

Whisk together peanut butter, honey, oil and chicken broth.

In a separate bowl, combine flours and oatmeal then mix dry ingredients into wet ingredients.

Place dough on lightly floured surface. Roll out to about ¼" inch thick.

Use a small bone cookie cutter to cut out cookies if you have one.

Roll out leftover scraps and cut out as many as you can. Put cookies on a parchment lined baking sheet and bake for 14-16 minutes. Turn off the oven and leave to cool inside for a crispy cookie.

Using bone shaped cookie cutters, cut the dough into shapes and transfer to parchment-lined baking sheets.

Bake for 10 to 12 minutes until golden brown. Cool completely before storing in an air tight container.

Paxi – Owned and photographed by Lie Florus

He looks stunning in any hat…

Liver Dog Treats

Ingredients

1½ lbs. liver (cut into small pieces)
½ cup whole wheat flour
2 eggs

Method

Preheat the oven to 350°

Puree the liver in a blender.

Add the flour and eggs, and process until smooth.

Spread evenly an 11x13 inch pan or your preferred size.

Bake for 15 minutes or until the center is firm.

Cool and cut into squares using a pizza cutter (treats will have a sponge like consistency).

Store in a sealed container in the refrigerator or freeze in bags.

Some things just fill your heart without trying...

Cranberry Bites

Ingredients

2 eggs
2 cups flour – you choose what sort of flour
1 tbsp coconut oil - melted
½ cup dried cranberries

Method

Preheat oven to 165°C.

Beat 2 eggs and set aside.

Combine the flour, coconut oil and dried cranberries together in a bowl.

Once combined, pour in the eggs and mix together well. You may have to use extra flour or add a little milk to get the right consistency.

Roll out your dough on a lightly floured board and cut out the treats using bite sized cookie cutters.

Place your treats on a lightly greased cookie sheet. Bake in the oven for 15-18 minutes or until crisp. Leave to cool.

A PETS PRAYER ~ Author Unknown

If it should be, that I grow frail and weak,
And pain should keep me from my sleep,
Then you must do what must be done
For this, the last battle, can't be won.

You will be sad, I understand.
Don't let your grief then stay your hand,
For this day, more than the rest,
Your love and friendship stand the test.

We've had so many happy years
What is to come can hold no fears.
You'd not want me to suffer, so,
When the time comes, please let me go.

Take me where my needs they'll tend only,
Stay with me to the end,
And hold me firm and speak to me,
Until my eyes no longer see.

I know in time you will see
It is a kindness you do to me
Although my tail its last has waved
From pain and suffering I've been saved.

Don't grieve that it should be you,
Who decides this thing to do
We've been so close these years
Don't let your heart hold any tears.

Smile - for we walked together.
And I will always be near you forever…

Banana and Peanut Butter Discs

Ingredients

1 banana, peeled
1 cup oat flour
2/3 cup rolled oats
½ cup dried parsley
3 tbsp peanut butter
1 egg, beaten

Method

Preheat oven to 300°.

Put banana in a large bowl and using a potato masher, mash it thoroughly.

Add the oat flour, oats, parsley, peanut butter and egg and mix well. Put in fridge for 5 minutes.

Roll mixture into small balls and place on lightly greased baking sheet.

Use a fork, press each ball into a 1½ to 2-inch coin.

Bake until firm and deep golden brown on the bottom, 40 to 45 minutes. Turn oven off and leave in to cool completely.

Store in airtight container for up to a week, freeze some for later too.

To Find Out Who is Your Best Friend...

1. Close Your Partner and Your Dog in the Trunk of your Car and Leave for 1 Minute

3. Open Trunk and Your Best Friend is the One Who is Pleased to See You - works every time...

Thank you

Finally I hope you have enjoyed this book – if you have, please tell your friends. It would make a great gift for your dog loving friends.

I have really enjoyed putting it together and trying out the recipes. I hope, together, we can help a few of the very deserving rescue charities that do such great work helping unwanted animals.

If you have a favourite charity you would like me to donate to, please send me an email and I will send a small donation on your behalf.

Email: **info@dogtreatrecipes.co.uk**

I would love to keep in touch and send you more Dog Treat Recipes as I find and try them. If you would like to join my mailing list, please add your email address

http://eepurl.com/bYgmcL or if you have a QR code reader on your phone here is the code to take you to the signup page.

"Dogs feel very strongly that they should always go with you in the car, in case the need should arise for them to bark violently at nothing right in your ear."

~ Dave Barry

Some Simple Conversion Figures

IMPERIAL TO METRIC

1 oz = 30g
4 oz = 110g
1lb   = 450g

1 fl.oz = 30ml
5 fl.oz or ¼ pt = 150ml
20 fl.oz or 1pt = 600ml

OVEN TEMPERATURES

130C = 110C fan = 250F = Gas mark 1
150C = 130C fan = 300F = Gas mark 2
170C = 150C fan = 325F = Gas mark 3
180C = 160C fan = 350F = Gas mark 4
190C = 170C fan = 375F = Gas mark 5
200C = 180C fan = 400F = Gas mark 6
220C = 200C fan = 425F = Gas mark 7
230C = 210C fan = 450F = Gas mark 8
240C = 220C fan = 475F = Gas mark 9

AMERICAN SPOON MEASURES

1 level tablespoon flour = 15g flour
1 heaped tablespoon flour = 28g flour
1 level tablespoon sugar = 28g sugar
1 level tablespoon butter = 15g butter

AMERICAN LIQUID MEASURES

1 cup US = 240ml
1 pint US = 480ml
1 quart US = 950ml

AMERICAN SOLID MEASURES

1 cup flour = 125g
1 cup butter = 225g
1 cup brown sugar = 170g
1 cup granulated sugar = 170g
1 cup icing sugar = 100g
1 cup uncooked rice = 170g
1 cup chopped nuts = 100g
1 cup fresh breadcrumbs = 150g
1 cup sultanas = 140g

DISCLAIMER

All information in the book is for general information purposes only.

The author has used her best efforts in preparing this information and makes no representations or warranties with respect to the accuracy, applicability or completeness of the material contained within.

The author shall in no event be held liable for losses or damages whatsoever. The author assumes no responsibility or liability for any consequences resulting directly or indirectly from any action or lack of action that you take based on the information in this document. Use of the publication and recipes therein is at your own risk.

Reproduction or translation of any part of this publication by any means, electronic or mechanical, without the permission of the author, is both forbidden and illegal. You are not permitted to share, sell, and trade or give away this document, it is for your own personal use only, unless stated otherwise.

The reader assumes full risk and responsibility for all actions taken as a result of the information contained within this book and the author will not be held responsible for any loss or damage, whether consequential, incidental, or otherwise that may result from the information presented in this book.

The author has relied on her own experiences when compiling this book and each recipe is tried and tested in her own kitchen.

By using any of the recipes in this publication, you agree that you have read the disclaimer and agree with all the terms.

Notes

16982977R00039

Printed in Great Britain
by Amazon